# You Can't Win Them All, Charlie Brown

Selected Cartoons from
"Ha Ha, Herman," Charlie Brown, Volume 2

## Charles M. Schulz

D0487362

**CORONET BOOKS**
Hodder Fawcett, London

First published 1975 by Fawcett Publications, Inc.,
New York

*Coronet edition 1976*
*Fourth impression 1978*

---

Printed in Great Britain for
Hodder Fawcett Ltd.,
Mill Road, Dunton Green, Sevenoaks, Kent
(Editorial Office, 47 Bedford Square,
London, WC1 3DP) by
C. Nicholls & Company Ltd,
The Philips Park Press, Manchester

ISBN 0 340 20754 X

type type type
DING!
type type type
type DING!
ZIP! BANG!
RATTLE RATTLE!
type type
type type.
DING!
type type type type DING!
fold fold fold, lick lick!
stamp stamp!
type type
?!*?! ZIP!
type type DING!
ON FRIDAY AFTERNOONS AT FOUR O'CLOCK, SECRETARIES MAKE A LOT OF NOISE!
ZOOM!
SCHULZ

I HOPE I HELPED HIM, BUT I DON'T KNOW...

TEN MINUTES BEFORE YOU GO TO A PARTY IS NO TIME TO BE LEARNING HOW TO DANCE!

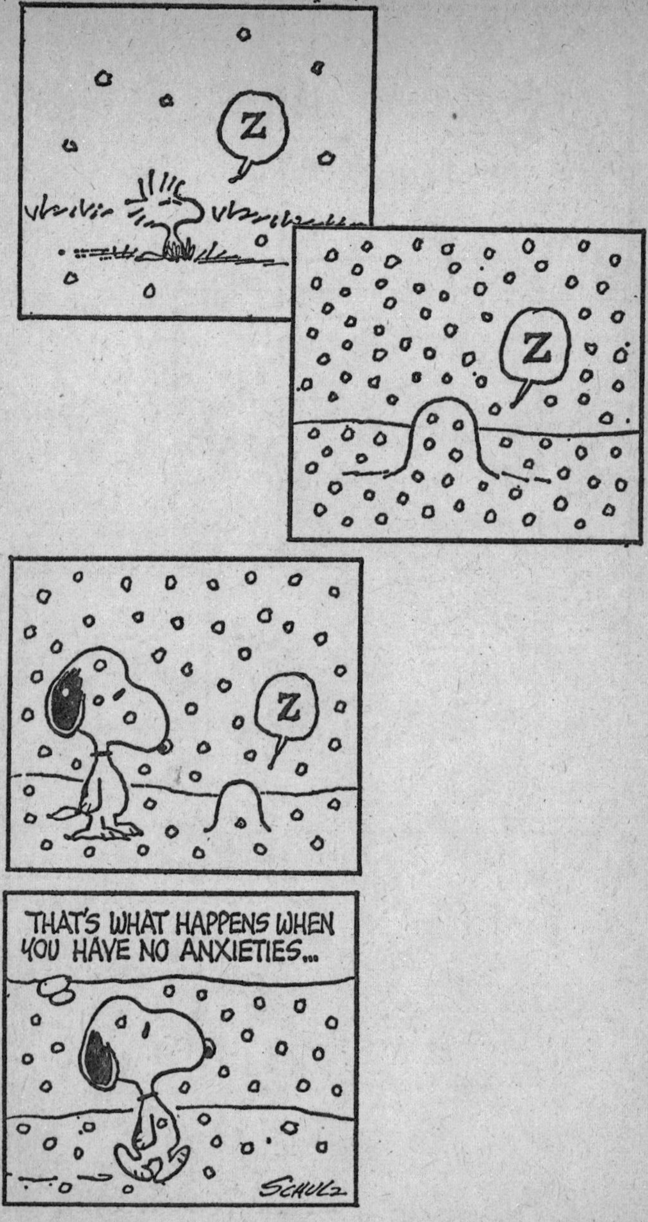
Z
Z
Z
THAT'S WHAT HAPPENS WHEN YOU HAVE NO ANXIETIES...
SCHULZ

Dear Santa Claus,
Do you need a secretary to help during the holiday season?
I could answer letters and run errands, and I will work for only five-hundred dollars a week.
FIVE HUNDRED DOLLARS A WEEK?!
WHY NOT? EVERYONE KNOWS THE OLD GUY IS LOADED!
SCHULZ

## THE WONDERFUL WORLD OF PEANUTS

*Numbers 1-25 and all the above Peanuts titles are available at your local bookshop or newsagent, or can be ordered direct from the publisher. Just tick the titles you want and fill in the form below.*
*Prices and availability subject to change without notice.*